I0889036

TABLE OF CONTENTS

Workbook Answers

Chapter 1 - Place Value and Number Sense

Pg 6

Pg 7			
No.	**Answer**	**No.**	**Answer**
1	even	13	odd
2	odd	14	even
3	even	15	even
4	even	16	even
5	odd	17	odd
6	even	18	odd
7	odd	19	even
8	odd	20	even
9	even	21	odd
10	odd	22	odd
11	odd	23	even
12	even	24	even

Pg 8		Pg 9		Pg 10		Pg 11	
No.	**Answer**	**No.**	**Answer**	**No.**	**Answer**	**No.**	**Answer**
1	odd	1	300	1	8,000	1	78
2	even	2	900	2	1,000	2	34
3	even	3	300	3	2,000	3	15
4	odd	4	100	4	9,000	4	2
5	odd	5	200	5	1,000	5	8
6	even	6	800	6	6,000	6	9
7	odd	7	800	7	4,000	7	3
8	even	8	100	8	9,000	8	5
9	even	9	800	9	2,000	9	89
10	even	10	400	10	7,000		
11	odd	11	300	11	2,000		
12	odd	12	300	12	5,000		
13	even	13	600	13	7,000		
14	odd	14	1,000	14	4,000		
15	odd	15	200	15	7,000		
16	even	16	300	16	9,000		
17	even	17	400	17	1,000		
18	even	18	700	18	5,000		
19	even	19	700	19	5,000		
20	even	20	500	20	2,000		
21	odd	21	200	21	2,000		
22	odd	22	800	22	1,000		
23	odd	23	300	23	2,000		
24	even	24	200	24	5,000		
		25	800	25	1,000		
		26	200	26	9,000		
		27	800	27	8,000		
		28	300	28	3,000		

Pg 12		Pg 13		Pg 14	
No.	**Answer**	**No.**	**Answer**	**No.**	**Answer**
1	24	1	129	1	1,347
2	43	2	235	2	3,232
3	39	3	254	3	2,459
4	66	4	325	4	4,157
5	59	5	507	5	3,175
6	86				

Pg 15	
No.	**Answer**
1	4,818 | 4,982 | 14,818
2	880 | 1,251 |1,900
3	1,210 | 1,541 | 1,780
4	50 | 74 | 129
5	815 | 1,520 | 3,500
6	3,400 | 5,800 | 9,570
7	10 | 100 | 1,000
8	5 | 300 | 4,500
9	250 | 275 | 300
10	16 | 25 | 54

Pg 16		Pg 17		Pg 18	
No.	**Answer**	**No.**	**Answer**	**No.**	**Answer**
1	>	1	>	1	1,221
2	>	2	<	2	2,142
3	<	3	=	3	333
4	<	4	>	4	3,321
5	<	5	>	5	2,340
6	=	6	>		
7	=	7	<		
8	<	8	<		
9	>	9	=		
10	<	10	<		
11	>	11	>		
12	<	12	<		
13	>	13	>		
14	=	14	=		
15	>	15	<		
16	>	16	<		
17	<	17	=		
18	=	18	>		
19	<	19	>		
20	<	20	<		

The place value of a digit is determined by where it is in a number.

Hundred Thousands	Ten Thousands	Thousands	Hundreds	Tens	Ones
1	2	3	4	5	6

123,456

One Hundred Twenty Three Thousand, Four Hundred Fifty Six

Write these numbers correctly in the blanks.

1. 392,599 =

3	9	2	5	9	9
Hundred Thousands	Ten Thousands	Thousands	Hundreds	Tens	Ones

2. 415,675 =

4	1	5	6	7	5
Hundred Thousands	Ten Thousands	Thousands	Hundreds	Tens	Ones

3. 726,211 =

7	2	6	2	1	1
Hundred Thousands	Ten Thousands	Thousands	Hundreds	Tens	Ones

4. 186,452 =

1	8	6	4	5	2
Hundred Thousands	Ten Thousands	Thousands	Hundreds	Tens	Ones

Pg 19

Chapter 2 – Addition

Pg 21		Pg 22		Pg 23	
No.	**Answer**	**No.**	**Answer**	**No.**	**Answer**
1	79	1	121	1	166
2	89	2	47	2	134
3	62	3	89	3	138
4	77	4	84	4	131
5	99	5	113	5	55
6	106	6	94	6	165
7	78	7	42	7	44
8	38	8	116	8	151
9	69	9	86	9	113
10	78	10	23	10	87
11	29	11	88	11	120
12	47	12	53	12	125
		13	91	13	84
		14	87	14	105
		15	128	15	25
		16	119	16	97
		17	86	17	60
		18	78	18	60
		19	120	19	77

Pg 24	
No.	**Answer**
1	100 + 10 + 10 + 1 = 121
2	100 + 1 + 1 + 1 + 1 + 1 = 105
3	100 + 100 + 100 + 100 + 100 + 10 = 510
4	10 + 10 + 10 + 10 + 1 + 1 = 42
5	100 + 100 + 10 + 10 + 10 + 10 = 240
6	100 + 10 + 1 + 1 + 1 +1 = 114
7	100 + 100 + 100 + 10 + 1 + 1 = 312
8	100 + 10 + 10 + 10 +10 + 1 = 141

Pg 25	
No.	**Answer**
1	1,000 + 100 + 10 + 1 + 1 = 1,112
2	1,000 + 1,000 + 1,000 + 100 + 1 = 3,101
3	1,000 + 100 + 100 + 10 + 1 + 1 = 1,212
4	1,000 + 1,000 + 1,000 + 1,000 + 100 = 4,100
5	1,000 + 1,000 + 100 + 100 + 10 + 10 = 2,220
6	100 + 10 + 10 + 1 + 1 + 1 = 123
7	1,000 + 1,000 + 100 + 10 + 10 + 1 = 2,121
8	100 + 100 + 100 + 10 + 10 + 1 = 321

Pg 26		Pg 27		Pg 28	
No.	**Answer**	**No.**	**Answer**	**No.**	**Answer**
1	1,806	1	1,773	1	2,387
2	892	2	2,782	2	1,190
3	1,330	3	851	3	3,055
4	923	4	1,437	4	2,254
5	1,322	5	1,648	5	1,569
6	831	6	1,286	6	2,266
7	389	7	899	7	1,619
8	1,054	8	1,208	8	2,094
9	1,580	9	2,228	9	1,536
10	204	10	1,511	10	2,321
11	964	11	1,054	11	1,485
12	876	12	1,947	12	1,481
13	1,364	13	1,673	13	1,038
14	648	14	1,395	14	1,833
15	714	15	722	15	1,182
16	1,030				
17	1,046				
18	562				
19	975				

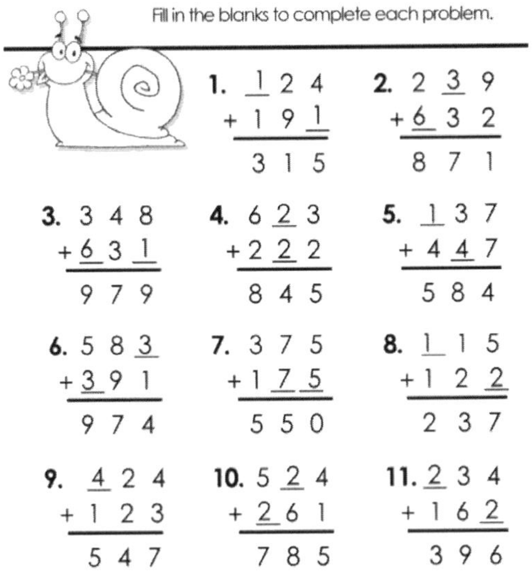
Fill in the blanks to complete each problem.

1. 124 + 191 = 315
2. 239 + 632 = 871
3. 348 + 631 = 979
4. 623 + 222 = 845
5. 137 + 447 = 584
6. 583 + 391 = 974
7. 375 + 175 = 550
8. 115 + 122 = 237
9. 424 + 123 = 547
10. 524 + 261 = 785
11. 234 + 162 = 396

Pg 29

Pg 30		Pg 31	
No.	**Answer**	**No.**	**Answer**
1	5,501	1	7,641
2	7,061	2	10,626
3	8,636	3	11,044
4	8,023	4	21,672
5	8,711	5	19,295
6	9,482	6	22,701
7	4,121	7	19,214
8	15,195	8	23,256
9	18,911	9	18,628
10	6,526	10	11,171
11	14,723	11	9,686
12	8,041	12	21,667
13	7,905		
14	10,164		
15	4,399		

- Add the numbers going down
- Add the numbers going across.
- Then add your answers together, either across or down, to fill in the the last square

3	4	7
2	3	5
5	7	(12)

1.

1	5	6
5	2	7
6	7	(13)

2.

2	8	10
8	9	17
10	17	(27)

3.

6	3	9
3	6	9
9	9	(18)

4.

2	15	17
15	2	17
17	17	(34)

5.

25	4	29
4	10	14
29	14	(43)

6.

1	8	9
8	40	48
9	48	(57)

Pg 32

- Add the numbers going down
- Add the numbers going across.
- Then add your answers together, either across or down, to fill in the the last square

3	4	7
2	3	5
5	7	(12)

1.

10	3	13
3	10	13
13	13	(26)

2.

5	8	13
8	5	13
13	13	(26)

3.

1	7	8
7	1	8
8	8	(16)

4.

3	6	9
6	12	18
9	18	(27)

5.

70	13	83
13	45	58
83	58	(141)

6.

2	36	38
36	2	38
38	38	(76)

Pg 33

Chapter 3 – Subtraction

Pg 35		Pg 36		Pg 37		Pg 38	
No.	**Answer**	**No.**	**Answer**	**No.**	**Answer**	**No.**	**Answer**
1	13	1	2	1	44	1	28
2	5	2	7	2	45	2	37
3	5	3	7	3	23	3	66
4	36	4	4	4	8	4	42
5	37	5	53	5	23	5	526
6	20	6	61	6	55	6	612
7	22	7	6	7	9	7	523
8	22	8	48	8	8	8	472
9	27	9	68	9	52	9	678
10	14	10	40	10	41	10	378
11	59	11	8	11	33	11	65
12	43	12	60	12	36	12	605
		13	35	13	28	13	341
		14	48	14	61	14	483
		15	17	15	35	15	157
		16	8	16	55	16	77
		17	36	17	2	17	361
		18	31	18	18	18	313
		19	14	19	30	19	87

Pg 39		Pg 40		Pg 41		Pg 42	
No.	**Answer**	**No.**	**Answer**	**No.**	**Answer**	**No.**	**Answer**
1	380	1	182	1	85	1	105
2	658	2	119	2	32	2	80
3	204	3	299	3	136	3	170
4	261	4	106	4	42	4	30
5	457	5	87	5	81	5	135
6	3	6	156	6	53	6	20
7	204	7	155	7	83	7	119
8	277	8	260	8	73	8	199
9	339	9	77	9	112	9	41
10	769	10	110	10	74	10	86
11	359	11	425	11	20	11	50
12	338	12	55	12	61	12	40
13	551	13	208	13	37	13	60
14	249	14	234	14	160	14	15
15	769	15	23	15	40	15	30
16	555	16	236	16	57	16	30
17	520	17	502	17	92	17	187
18	166	18	592	18	16	18	75
19	794	19	104	19	356	19	180
				20	30	20	161

Pg 43		Pg 44		Pg 45		Pg 46	
No.	Answer	No.	Answer	No.	Answer	No.	Answer
1	194	1	2,071	1	3,366	1	1,889
2	591	2	2,009	2	904	2	4,267
3	122	3	8,920	3	2,459	3	1,044
4	793	4	2,980	4	154	4	2,589
5	377	5	3,331	5	861	5	3,679
6	881	6	4,091	6	1,248	6	19
7	587	7	5,071	7	3,761	7	889
8	314	8	4,334	8	3,626	8	489
9	233	9	2,781	9	5,071	9	1,175
10	195	10	5,565	10	1,925	10	2,689
11	619	11	7,573	11	2,075	11	1,230
12	214	12	1,121	12	111	12	6,495
13	55	13	1,213	13	3,454	13	3,353
14	66	14	1,151	14	320	14	3,984
15	378						
16	46						
17	473						
18	95						
19	66						

Pg 47	
No.	Answer
1	4,690
2	5,844
3	2,045
4	2,571
5	1,784
6	4,222
7	5,406
8	5,897
9	6,122
10	5,009
11	5,329
12	408
13	9,036
14	676

Chapter 4 - Division

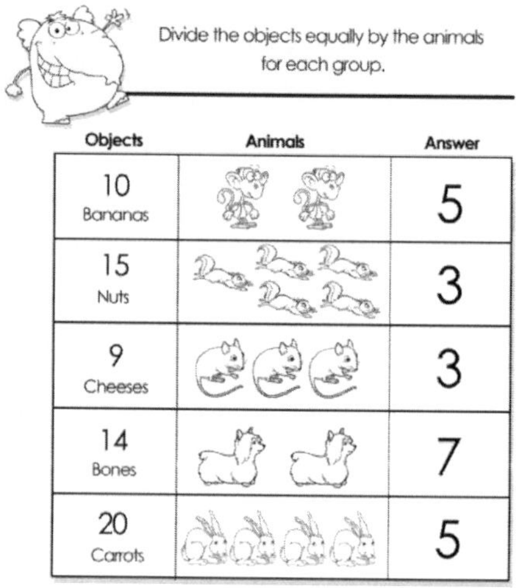
Divide the objects equally by the animals for each group.

Objects	Animals	Answer
10 Bananas		5
15 Nuts		3
9 Cheeses		3
14 Bones		7
20 Carrots		5

Pg 50

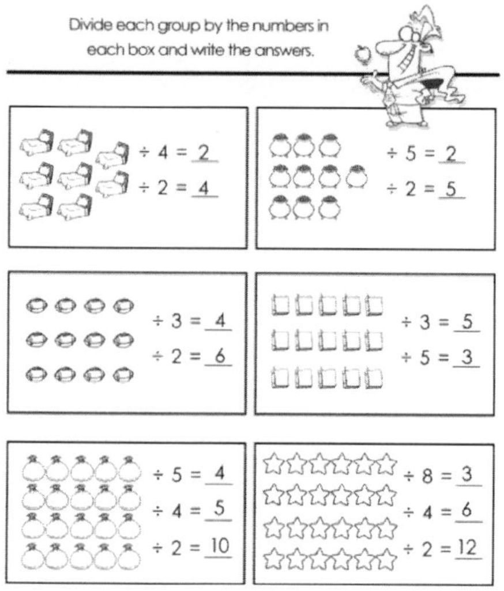
Divide each group by the numbers in each box and write the answers.

÷ 4 = 2
÷ 2 = 4

÷ 5 = 2
÷ 2 = 5

÷ 3 = 4
÷ 2 = 6

÷ 3 = 5
÷ 5 = 3

÷ 5 = 4
÷ 4 = 5
÷ 2 = 10

÷ 8 = 3
÷ 4 = 6
÷ 2 = 12

Pg 51

Pg 52	
No.	**Answer**
1	18, 9, 2
2	16, 4, 4
3	125, 5, 25
4	15, 3, 5
5	100, 10, 10
6	72, 9, 8
7	4, 12, 3
8	5, 30, 6
9	6, 42, 7
10	8, 64, 8
11	2, 10, 5
12	3, 21, 7

Pg 53		Pg 54		Pg 55	
No.	**Answer**	**No.**	**Answer**	**No.**	**Answer**
1	7	1	$24 \div 8 = 3$, $24 \div 6 = 4$	1	6
2	7	2	$15 \div 3 = 5$, $15 \div 5 = 3$	2	5
3	46	3	$10 \div 2 = 5$, $10 \div 5 = 2$	3	6
4	52	4	$50 \div 5 = 10$, $50 \div 10 = 5$	4	4
5	28			5	4
6	37			6	9
7	27			7	8
8	33			8	9
9	22			9	8
10	99			10	8
11	59				
12	82				
13	80				
14	90				
15	30				
16	97				
17	46				
18	95				
19	59				
20	65				

Pg 56		Pg 57		Pg 58		Pg 59	
No.	**Answer**	**No.**	**Answer**	**No.**	**Answer**	**No.**	**Answer**
1	10	1	20	1	8	1	14
2	4	2	4	2	18	2	5
3	5	3	25	3	10	3	7
4	5	4	15	4	6	4	10
5	7	5	6	5	3	5	7
6	1	6	10	6	4	6	9
7	5	7	5	7	2	7	18
8	10	8	25	8	10	8	10
9	3	9	19	9	7	9	5
10	6	10	12	10	5	10	4
		11	22	11	17	11	36
		12	30	12	6	12	6
		13	10	13	13	13	10
		14	42	14	18	14	36
		15	6	15	21	15	5
		16	18	16	40	16	7
						17	100
						18	10
						19	40
						20	15

Pg 60	
No.	Answer
1	30
2	5
3	63
4	29
5	2
6	7
7	48
8	5
9	4
10	3
11	92
12	9
13	10
14	55
15	6
16	8
17	22
18	7
19	14
20	16

Chapter 5 – Fractions

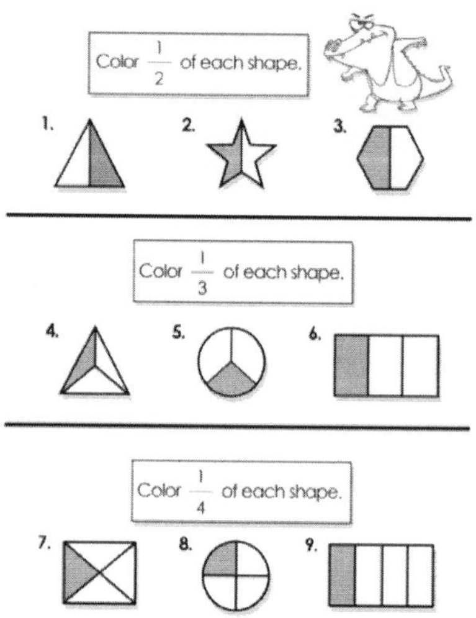

Pg 63

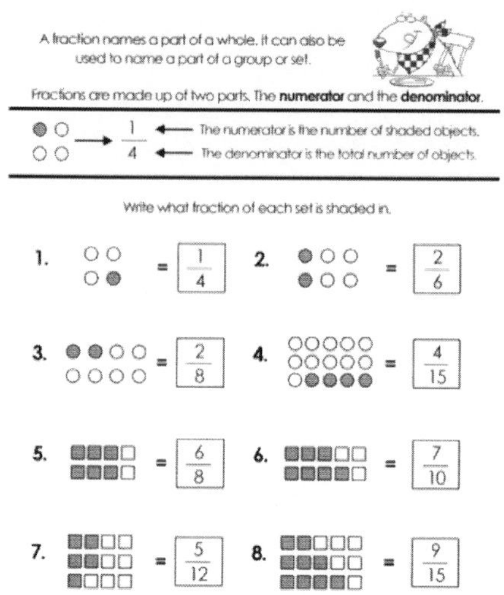

Pg 64

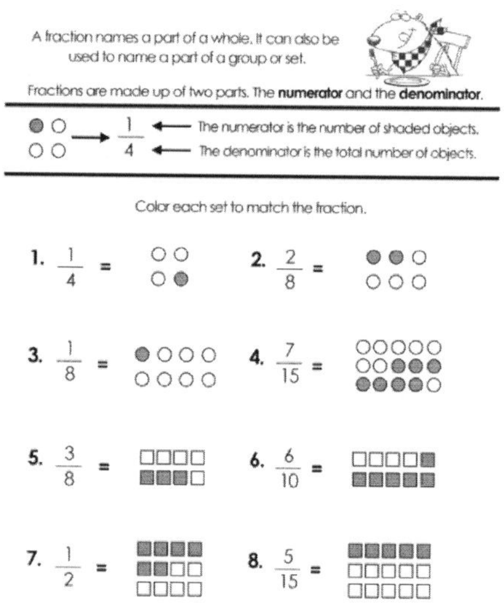

Pg 65

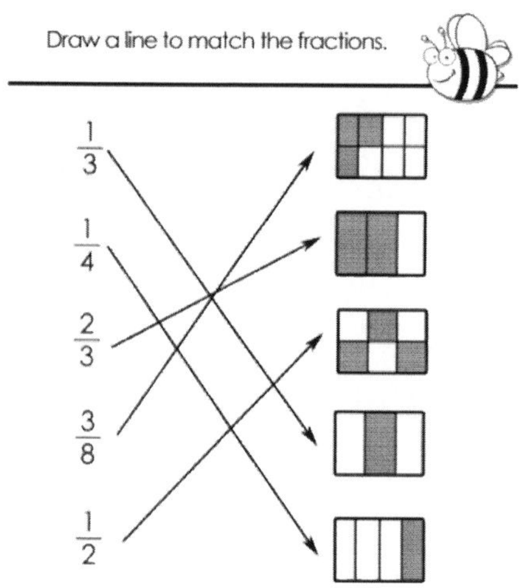

Pg 66

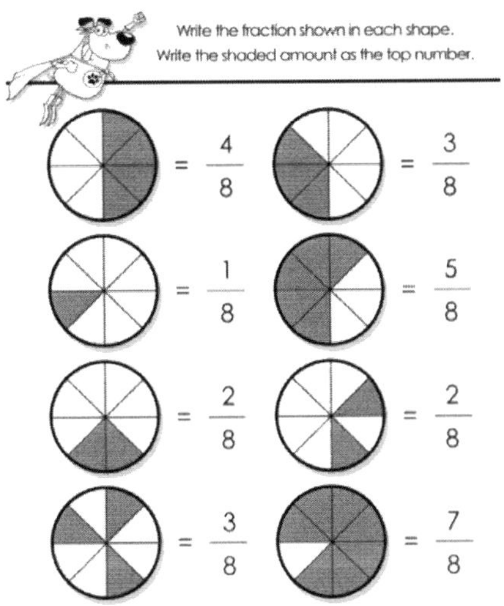

Pg 67

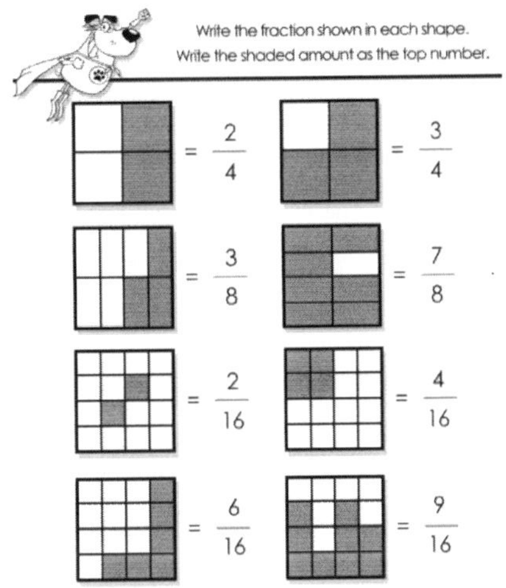

Pg 68

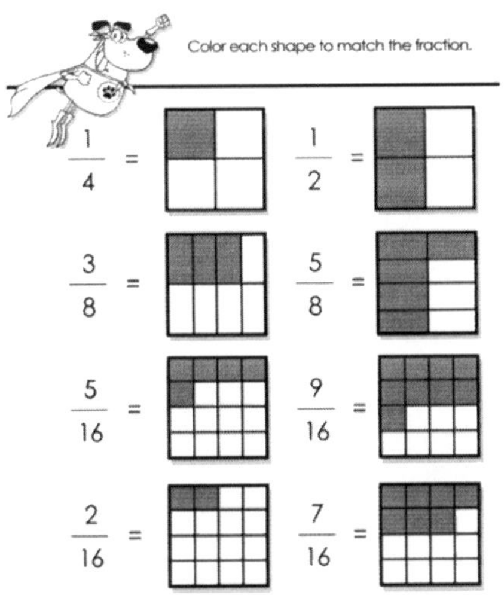

Pg 69

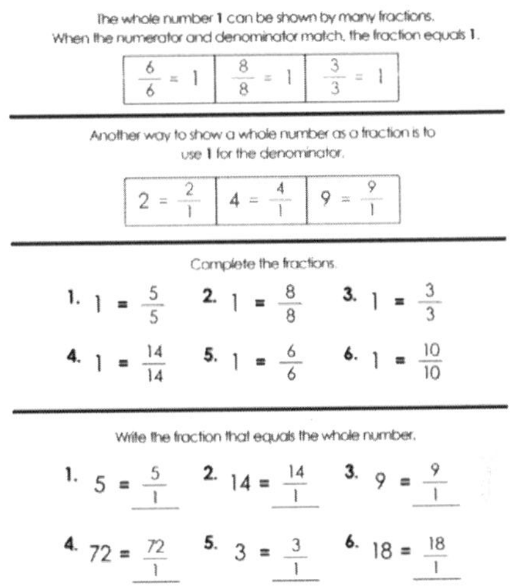

Pg 70

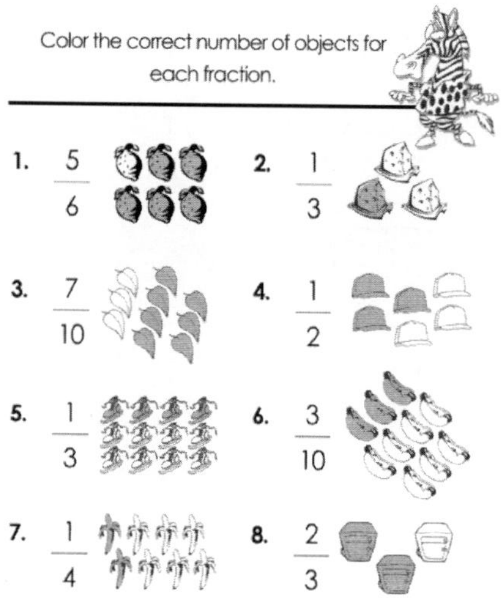

Pg 71

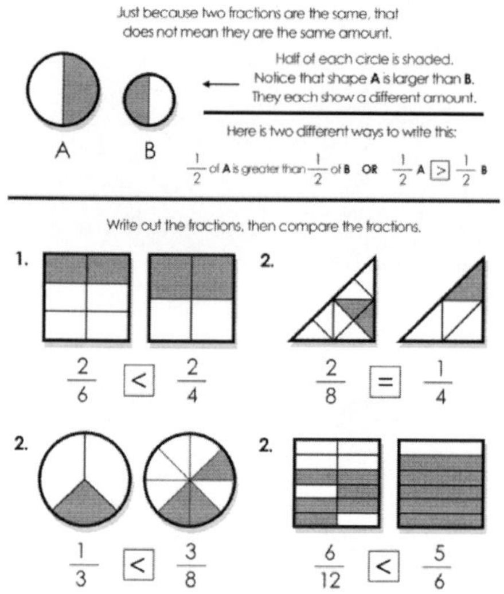

Pg 72

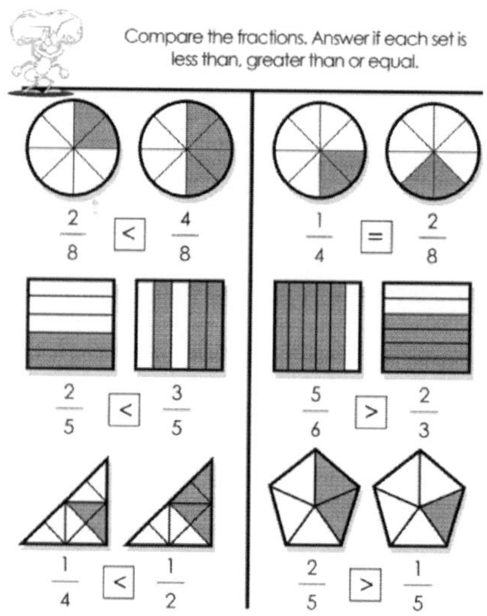

Pg 73

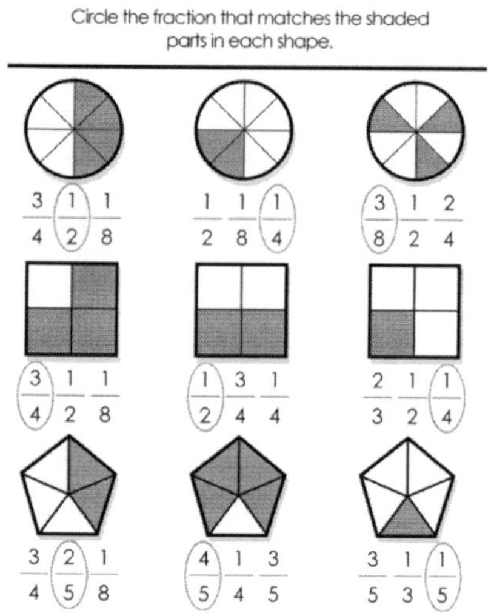

Pg 74

Chapter 6 – Multiplication

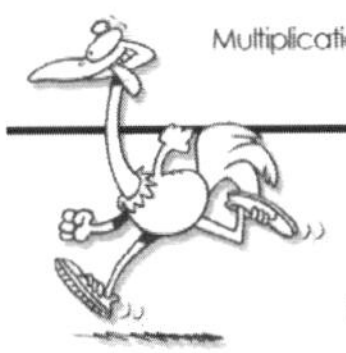

Multiplication is the way we find the sum of the same number a certain amount of times.

4 x 2 = 8
2 + 2 + 2 + 2 = 8

2 x 5 = 10
5 + 5 = 10

Break each group down by writing them out, then adding them together.

1. 3 x 2 = 6
2 + 2 + 2 = 6

2. 3 x 4 = 12
4 + 4 + 4 = 12

3. 4 x 4 = 16
4 + 4 + 4 + 4 = 16

4. 4 x 5 = 20
5 + 5 + 5 + 5 = 20

5. 3 x 8 = 24
8 + 8 + 8 = 24

6. 4 x 10 = 40
10 + 10 + 10 + 10 = 40

5. 2 x 6 = 12
6 + 6 = 12

6. 3 x 6 = 18
6 + 6 + 6 = 18

Pg 76

Pg 77			
No.	**Answer**	**No.**	**Answer**
1	0	12	4
2	4	13	6
3	1	14	5
4	9	15	3
5	9	16	0
6	6	17	2
7	2	18	7
8	8	19	8
9	6	20	7
10	0	21	0
11	3		

Pg 78		Pg 79		Pg 80		Pg 81	
No.	**Answer**	**No.**	**Answer**	**No.**	**Answer**	**No.**	**Answer**
1	18	1	6	1	3	1	12
2	8	2	0	2	0	2	10
3	16	3	4	3	20	3	35
4	7	4	14	4	12	4	18
5	18	5	24	5	4	5	0
6	10	6	12	6	16	6	5
7	7	7	18	7	0	7	18
8	4	8	24	8	28	8	40
9	6	9	0	9	8	9	0
10	6	10	16	10	2	10	16
11	18	11	27	11	36	11	30
12	8	12	21	12	20	12	25
13	14	13	0	13	32	13	4
14	10	14	9	14	4	14	45
15	0	15	2	15	0	15	18
16	12	16	7	16	24	16	16
17	16	17	0	17	18	17	0
18	0	18	15	18	27	18	15
19	4	19	9	19	12	19	9
20	2	20	15	20	12	20	10
21	8	21	18	21	27	21	18

Pg 82		Pg 83		Pg 84		Pg 85	
No.	**Answer**	**No.**	**Answer**	**No.**	**Answer**	**No.**	**Answer**
1	0	1	12	1	56	1	9
2	54	2	0	2	16	2	36
3	15	3	20	3	8	3	56
4	8	4	3	4	12	4	81
5	12	5	42	5	0	5	21
6	6	6	14	6	35	6	40
7	14	7	9	7	72	7	9
8	18	8	21	8	15	8	3
9	36	9	63	9	24	9	24
10	4	10	24	10	0	10	2
11	30	11	28	11	16	11	54
12	24	12	30	12	25	12	16
13	0	13	4	13	16	13	35
14	25	14	35	14	56	14	45
15	27	15	14	15	40	15	36
16	12	16	42	16	72	16	36
17	30	17	7	17	64	17	0
18	15	18	49	18	32	18	18
19	48	19	56	19	32	19	21
20	42	20	7	20	10	20	10
21	0	21	42	21	24	21	27

Pg 86		Pg 87		Pg 88		Pg 89	
No.	**Answer**	**No.**	**Answer**	**No.**	**Answer**	**No.**	**Answer**
1	3	1	30	1	400	1	48
2	4	2	20	2	200	2	219
3	5	3	50	3	500	3	120
4	9	4	60	4	600	4	128
5	6	5	10	5	100	5	48
6	2	6	50	6	400	6	63
7	10	7	40	7	800	7	75
8	8	8	80	8	900	8	108
9	6	9	70	9	0	9	49
10	7	10	0	10	700	10	76
		11	90	11	300		
		12	20	12	700		
		13	40	13	400		
		14	30	14	300		
		15	90	15	900		

Chapter 7 – Graphing

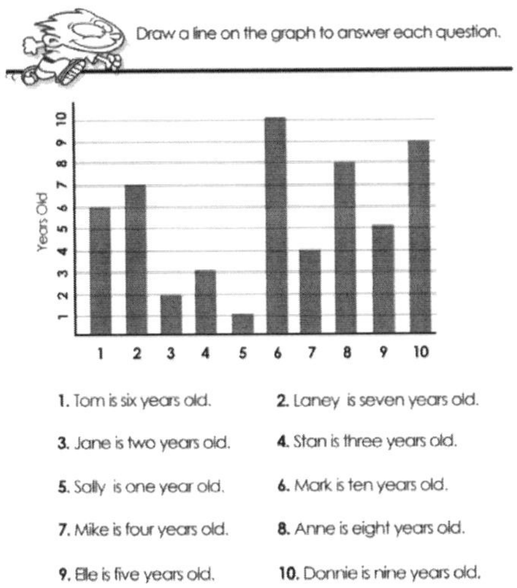
Draw a line on the graph to answer each question.

1. Tom is six years old.
2. Laney is seven years old.
3. Jane is two years old.
4. Stan is three years old.
5. Sally is one year old.
6. Mark is ten years old.
7. Mike is four years old.
8. Anne is eight years old.
9. Elle is five years old.
10. Donnie is nine years old.

Pg 91

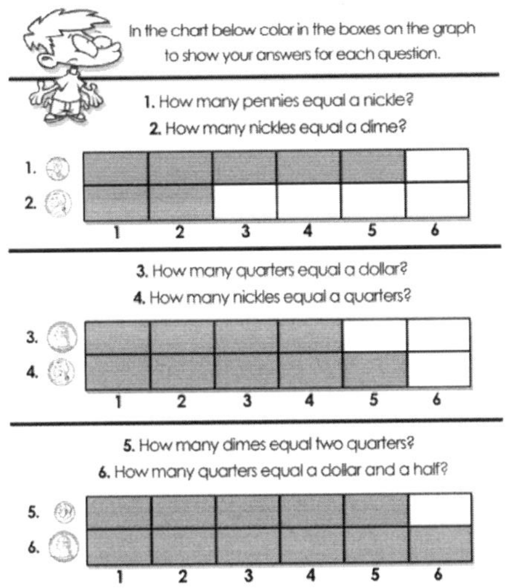
In the chart below color in the boxes on the graph to show your answers for each question.

1. How many pennies equal a nickle?
2. How many nickles equal a dime?

3. How many quarters equal a dollar?
4. How many nickles equal a quarters?

5. How many dimes equal two quarters?
6. How many quarters equal a dollar and a half?

Pg 92

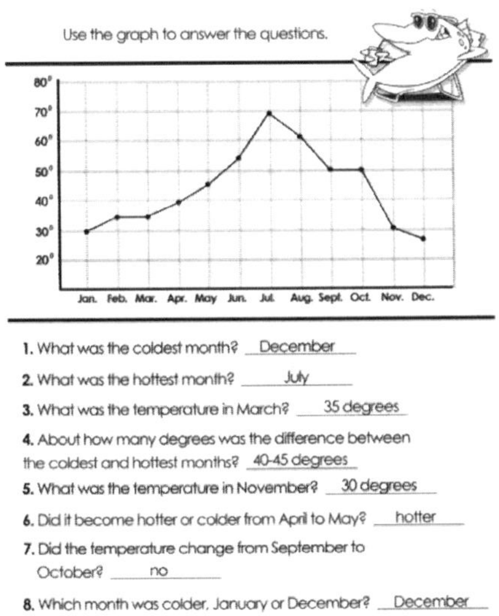
Use the graph to answer the questions.

1. What was the coldest month? December
2. What was the hottest month? July
3. What was the temperature in March? 35 degrees
4. About how many degrees was the difference between the coldest and hottest months? 40-45 degrees
5. What was the temperature in November? 30 degrees
6. Did it become hotter or colder from April to May? hotter
7. Did the temperature change from September to October? no
8. Which month was colder, January or December? December

Pg 93

Pg 95	
No.	**Answer**
1	pancakes
2	ham
3	bacon
4	ham
5	bacon
6	pancakes
7	eggs

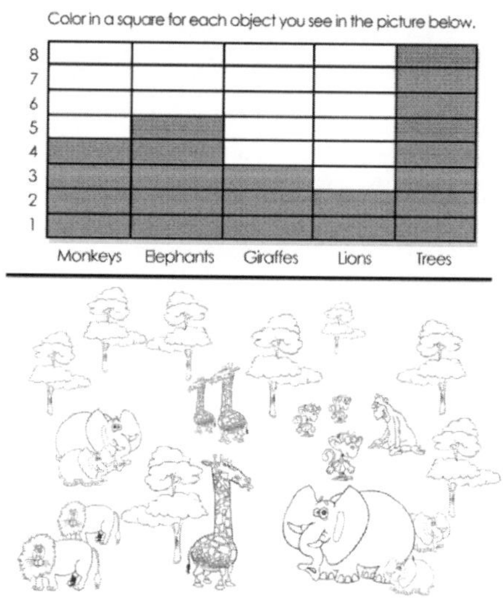

Pg 96

Pg 97		Pg 98	
No.	**Answer**	**No.**	**Answer**
1	3	1	$50
2	5	2	13 miles
3	2	3	32 pieces of candy
4	4	4	97 cupcakes
5	5		
6	1		
7	6		

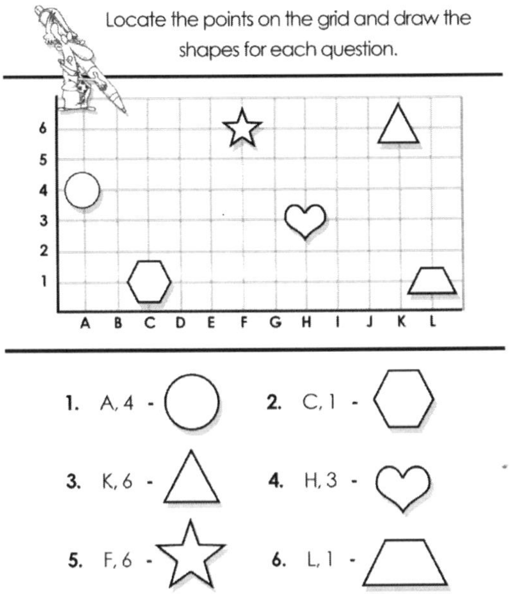
Locate the points on the grid and draw the shapes for each question.
6
5
4
3
2
1
A B C D E F G H I J K L
1. A, 4 -
2. C, 1 -
3. K, 6 -
4. H, 3 -
5. F, 6 -
6. L, 1 -

Pg 99

Chapter 8 - Money & Time

Pg 103		Pg 104		Pg 105		Pg 106	
No.	**Answer**	**No.**	**Answer**	**No.**	**Answer**	**No.**	**Answer**
1	76¢	1	$1.41	1	25¢	1	$3.95
2	72¢	2	$3.12	2	23¢	2	$2.39
3	$1.55	3	$7.61	3	36¢	3	$1.68
4	$1.86	4	$30.18	4	52¢	4	$4.39
5	93¢	5	$25.87	5	$3.93	5	$3.91
6	$1.81	6	$35.33	6	$3.64	6	$6.79
7	$1.36			7	$4.36	7	$9.19
8	$1.09					8	$13.20
9	$1.45						

Pg 107	
No.	**Answer**
1	thirty-eight dollars and fifty-nine cents
2	one-hundred dollars and thirty-two cents
3	two-hundred seventy-eight dollars and twelve cents
4	three-hundred fifteen dollars and eight cents
5	nine-hundred fifteen dollars and eighty-three cents
6	eighteen dollars and thirty-three cents
7	two-hundred twenty-nine dollars and twenty-nine cents
8	seven-hundred fifty-six dollars and ten cents
9	six-hundred eighteen dollars and twenty-four cents
10	nine-hundred ninety-nine dollars and seventy-two cents

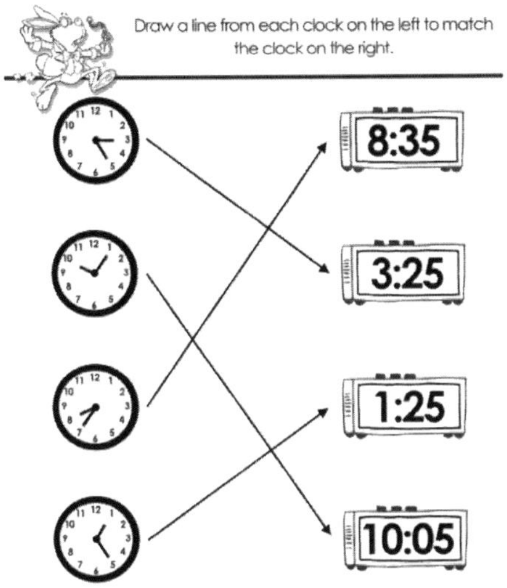

Pg 109

Pg 110		Pg 111	
No.	**Answer**	**No.**	**Answer**
1	AM	1	6 hours 45 minutes
2	PM	2	9 hours 26 minutes
3	AM	3	5 hours 12 minutes
4	PM	4	15 hours 52 minutes
5	PM	5	3 hours 45 minutes
6	AM	6	1 hour 54 minutes
7	PM	7	58 minutes
8	PM	8	3 hours 48 minutes
9	AM		
10	PM		

Write the correct times in the clocks on the right.
9:15
What time will it be in 3 hours and 15 minutes?
10:30
What time will it be in 2 hours and 30 minutes?
11:45
What time will it be in 1 hour and 45 minutes?
4:45
What time will it be in 2 hours and 15 minutes?
5:15
What time will it be in 4 hours and 45 minutes?
8:45
What time will it be in 3 hours and 30 minutes?
8:45
What time will it be in 5 hours and 45 minutes?
9:45
What time will it be in 1 hour and 15 minutes?

Pg 112

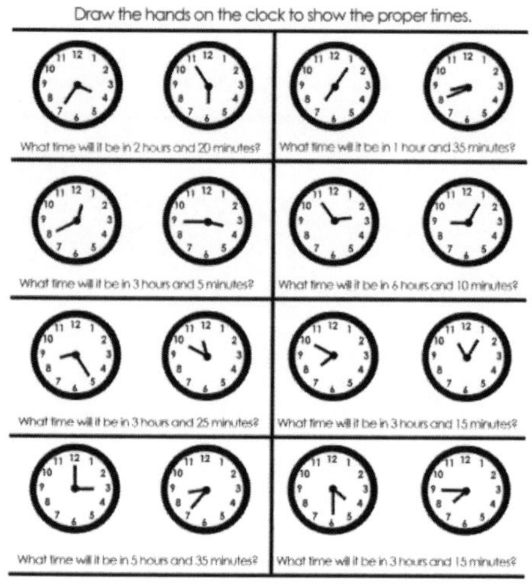
Draw the hands on the clock to show the proper times.
What time will it be in 2 hours and 20 minutes?
What time will it be in 1 hour and 35 minutes?
What time will it be in 3 hours and 5 minutes?
What time will it be in 6 hours and 10 minutes?
What time will it be in 3 hours and 25 minutes?
What time will it be in 3 hours and 15 minutes?
What time will it be in 5 hours and 35 minutes?
What time will it be in 3 hours and 15 minutes?

Pg 113

Chapter 9 - Geometry & Measurements

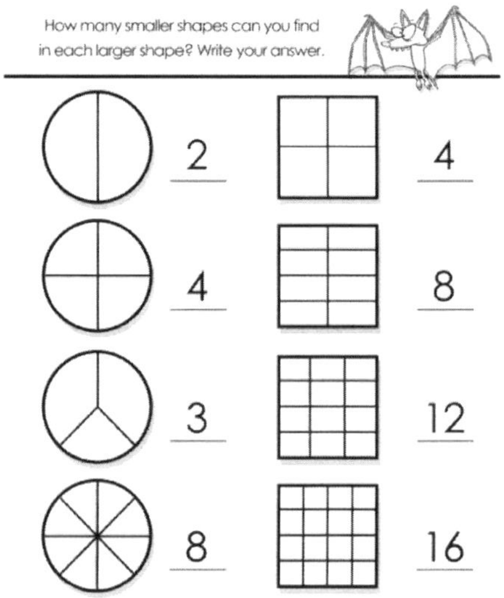

Pg 116

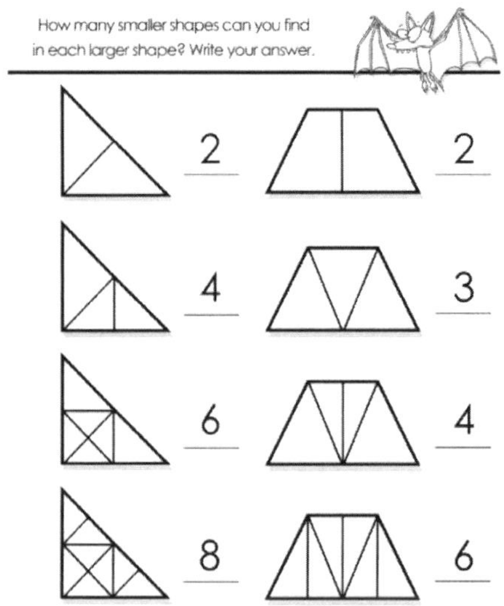

Pg 117

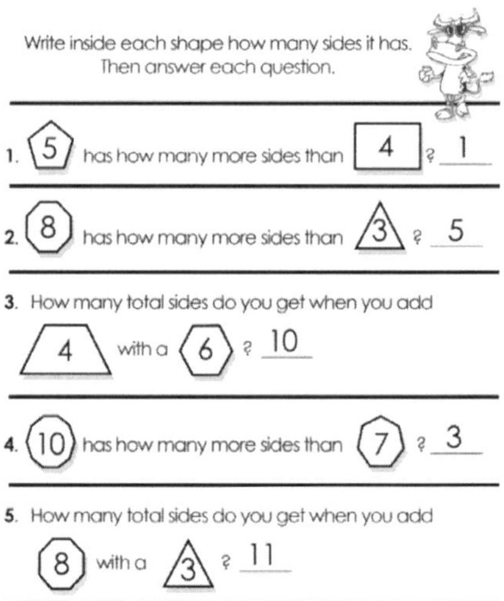

Pg 118

Pg 119	
No.	**Answer**
1	3
2	4
3	6
4	7
5	4
6	7
7	7
8	6

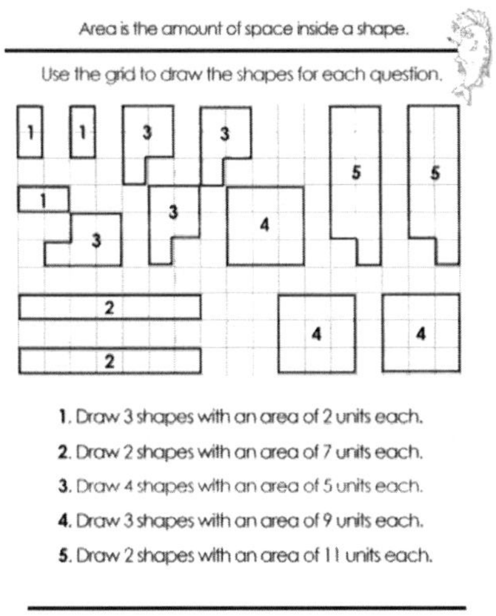

Pg 120

Pg 121		Pg 122	
No.	**Answer**	**No.**	**Answer**
1	4 + 6 + 4 +6 = 20 in	1	8
2	7 + 7 + 7 = 21ft	2	10
3	8 + 20 + 20 + 26 = 74in	3	9
4	12 + 8 + 12 + 8 = 40ft	4	12
5	6 + 6 + 9 +6 + 9 = 36in	5	10
6	3 + 3 + 3 + 3 + 3 + 3 = 18ft	6	12
		7	14
		8	14

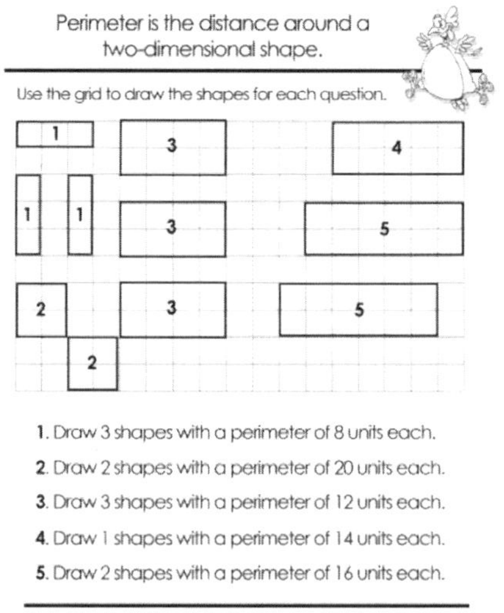
Perimeter is the distance around a two-dimensional shape.

Use the grid to draw the shapes for each question.

1. Draw 3 shapes with a perimeter of 8 units each.
2. Draw 2 shapes with a perimeter of 20 units each.
3. Draw 3 shapes with a perimeter of 12 units each.
4. Draw 1 shapes with a perimeter of 14 units each.
5. Draw 2 shapes with a perimeter of 16 units each.

Pg 123
Answers can vary

Pg 124			
No.	**Answer**	**No.**	**Answer**
1	line segment	1	XY or DF
2	point	2	line segment
3	line	3	any point on the illustration
4	line segment	4	line
		5	E

Pg 125		Pg 126		Pg 127		Pg 128	
No.	**Answer**	**No.**	**Answer**	**No.**	**Answer**	**No.**	**Answer**
1	obtuse	1	Ounces	1	yards	1	cup
2	acute	2	Pounds	2	feet	2	gallon
3	right	3	Ounces	3	miles	3	pint
4	obtuse	4	Pounds	4	feet	4	quart
		5	Pounds	5	feet	5	pint
		6	Ounces	6	miles	6	gallon
				7	feet		
				8	yards		
				9	miles		
				10	foot		

Practice Test Answers

Practice Test #1

Answers and Explanations

1. C: You can think of 6×4 as six groups of four objects. If you buy 6 binders for $4 each, then the total amount of money you spend is $4 + $4 + $4 + $4 + $4 + $4, which is six groups of $4.

2. A: You can think of $24 \div 8$ as equally dividing 24 objects into eight groups. If 24 slices of pizza are divided between 8 people, then you have to divide the slices into eight groups.

3. B: There are 32 crayons that are evenly divided among 8 students. Therefore, you can find number of crayons each student gets by dividing 32 by 8. The result is 4 crayons each.

4. B: The opposite of multiplication is division. Use division of the product (20) by the known factor (4) to obtain the missing number.
Therefore, $20 \div 4 = 5$

5. D: The commutative property of multiplication states that the order of the numbers being multiplied does not matter. For instance, 2×3 and 3×2 are both equal to 6. In the problem, we are given the equation $9 \times 15 = 135$. Therefore, by the commutative property, 15×9 is also equal to 135.

6. C: Division and multiplication are inverse operations, just as subtraction and addition are. To calculate $7 - 3$, ask yourself "What number can be added to 3 to get 7?" Since the answer is 4, we know that $7 - 3 = 4$.

Similarly, to calculate $24 \div 6$, ask yourself "What number can be multiplied by 6 to get 24?" By trial-and-error, you can find that $4 \times 6 = 24$. Therefore, we know that $24 \div 6 = 4$.

7. D: In the multiplication table, the 8s are 8, 16, 24, 32, 40, 48, 56, 64, 72, 80. Therefore, $8 \times 9 = 72$.

8. D: To start, let the letter a stand for the amount of money Leslie had before she bought the ice cream (which is what we are looking for). Now we can say that after she spends $4 on ice cream, Leslie has a total of $a - 4$ dollars left. We are also told that she has $7 left after buying ice cream. Therefore, the correct equation is $a - 4 = 7$.

Because addition and subtraction are related, we can calculate a by adding $7 + 4$. The answer is 11, which we can check by making sure that $11 - 4 = 7$. It works, so Leslie had $11 before she bought the ice cream.

9. B: To start, let the letter b stand for price of each raffle ticket (which is what we are looking for). Now we can say that if you buy 7 raffle tickets, then the total price is $b \times 7$. We are also told that you spend a total of $21. Therefore, the correct equation is $b \times 7 = 21$.

Because multiplication and division are related, we can calculate b by dividing $21 \div 7$. The answer is 3, which we can check by making sure that $3 \times 7 = 21$. It works, so each raffle ticket cost $3.

10. B: Carefully examine the multiplication table and identify some of the products that are odd. For example:

$3 \times 3 = 9$
$3 \times 5 = 15$
$5 \times 1 = 5$
$7 \times 9 = 63$

Notice that in all of these cases the numbers being multiplied together are both odd.

11. C: To round to the nearest ten, first look at the digit in the tens place, which is a 3. Thus, if you round 437 *down*, the 3 will stay the same, and the answer will be 430. Conversely, if you round it *up*, the 3 will go up to a 4, and the answer will be 440. Finally, look at the number after the 3, which is a 7. Since it is greater than 5, you should round up. Therefore, the answer is 440.

12. B: Set up the addition vertically, making sure to line up the digits by place value.

$$\begin{array}{r} 381 \\ +\ 54 \\ \hline 435 \end{array}$$

13. D: Notice that 60 is a multiple of 10; in other words, it has a zero in the ones place. There is a trick to multiplying numbers like this. To multiply 4×60, first multiply 4×6 and then add a zero to the end. Therefore, the answer is 240.

14. A: A fraction $\frac{1}{b}$ can be represented as a whole partitioned (or divided) into b equal parts. For example, if a figure is divided into 2 equal parts, then each part represents $\frac{1}{2}$ of the whole. Notice that the rectangle in the problem is divided into 5 equal parts and one of those parts is shaded. Therefore, it represents the fraction $\frac{1}{5}$.

15. B: If you partition (or divide) the space between 0 and 1 on a number line into b equal parts, then each part has size $\frac{1}{b}$, and the first division to the right of zero represents the point $\frac{1}{b}$. For example, if you divide the space between 0 and 1 on a number line into three equal parts, then each part has size $\frac{1}{3}$ and the first endpoint represents the point $\frac{1}{3}$.

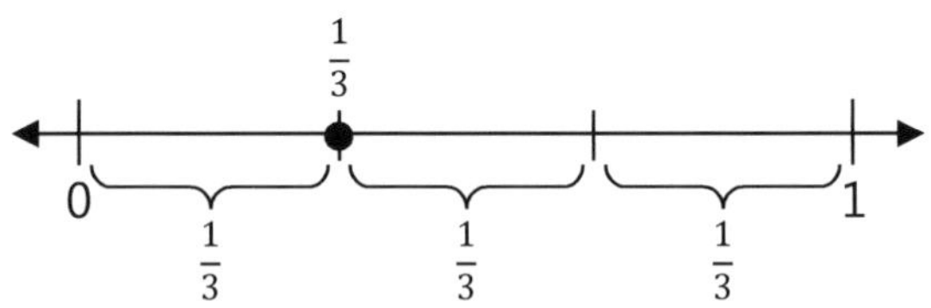

Therefore, to find $\frac{1}{4}$, divide the space between 0 and 1 on a number line into four equal parts. The first endpoint represents $\frac{1}{4}$.

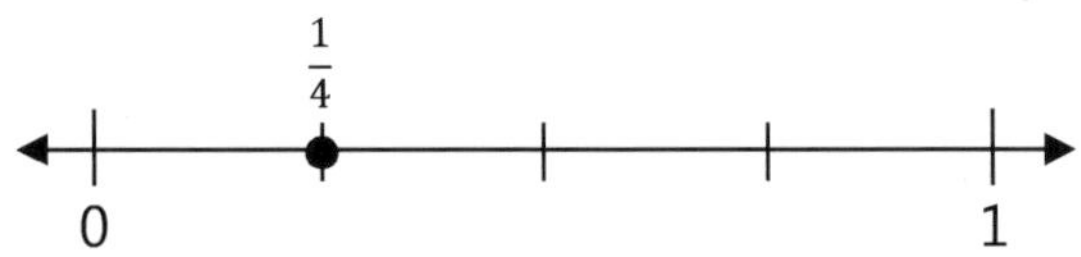

16. D: If you partition (or divide) the space between 0 and 1 on a number line into b equal parts, then the ath division to the right of zero is the point $\frac{a}{b}$. For example, if you divide the space between 0 and 1 on a number line into three equal parts, then the second endpoint represents the point $\frac{2}{3}$.

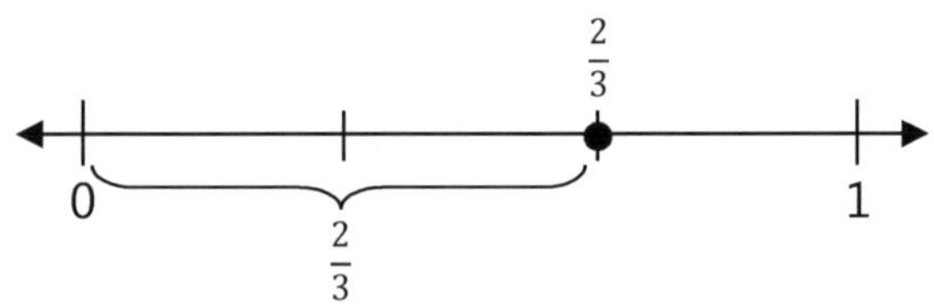

Therefore, to find $\frac{3}{5}$, divide the space between 0 and 1 on a number line into five equal parts. The third endpoint represents $\frac{3}{5}$.

17. B: A fraction can be represented as a whole partitioned (or divided) into equal parts. In addition, two fractions are equivalent if they are the same size. Notice that the circle in the problem is divided into 8 equal parts and two of those parts are shaded. Therefore, the shaded region represents $\frac{2}{8}$. This is equivalent to the fraction $\frac{1}{4}$ as shown by the darkly shaded area in the circles below.

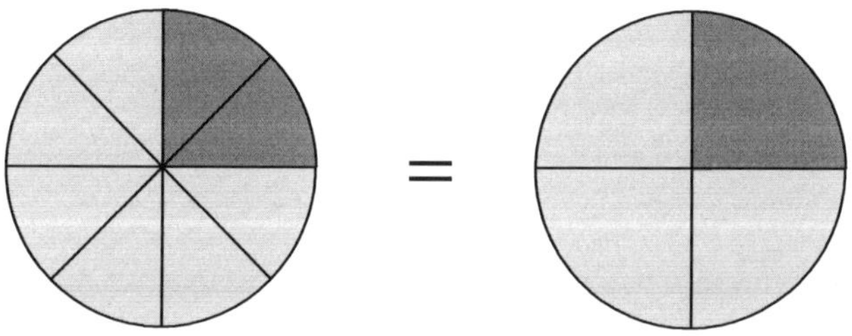

18. C: A fraction can be represented as a whole partitioned (or divided) into equal parts. In addition, two fractions are equivalent if they are the same size. The darkly shaded area below represents the fraction $\frac{4}{6}$.

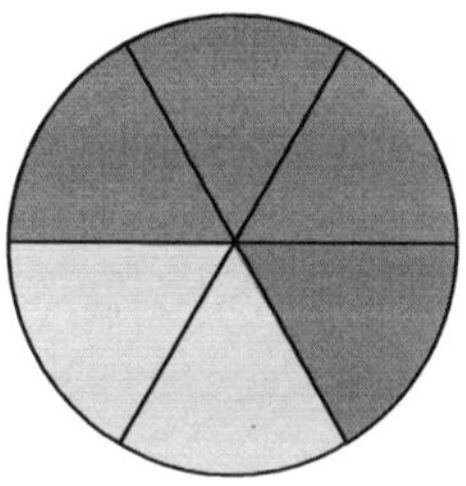

This is equivalent to the fraction $\frac{2}{3}$ as shown by the darkly shaded area below.

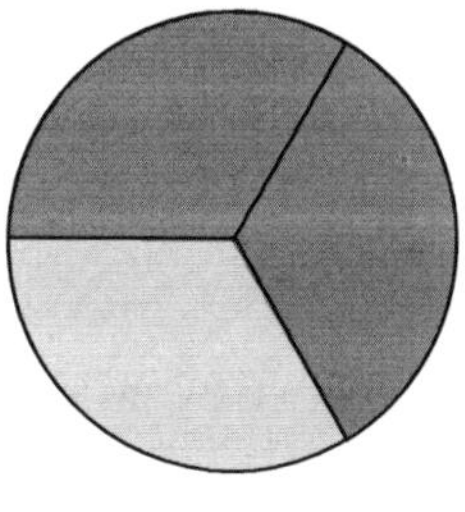

19. D: A whole number *a* can be expressed as a fraction $\frac{a}{1}$. This is because $\frac{a}{1}$ represents *a* "divided" into one part. Therefore, 5 is equivalent to the fraction $\frac{5}{1}$.

20. A: A fraction $\frac{a}{b}$ can be represented as *a* parts of a whole that is partitioned (or divided) into *b* equal parts. Therefore, if you divide a whole into 5 parts, then 3 of those parts are larger than 2 of them. Thus, the correct answer is $\frac{3}{5} > \frac{2}{5}$ as shown by the figures below.

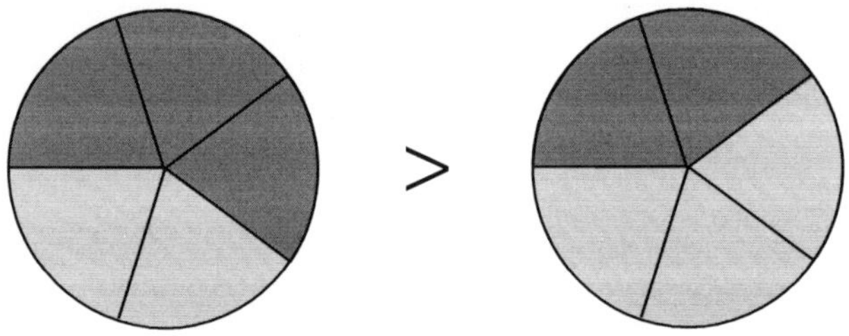

21. A: A fraction $\frac{a}{b}$ can be represented as *a* parts of a whole that is partitioned (or divided) into *b* equal parts. Therefore, if you divide a whole into 5 parts, then each part will be larger than if you had divided the whole into 7 parts. Thus, the correct answer is $\frac{2}{5} > \frac{2}{7}$ as shown by the figures below.

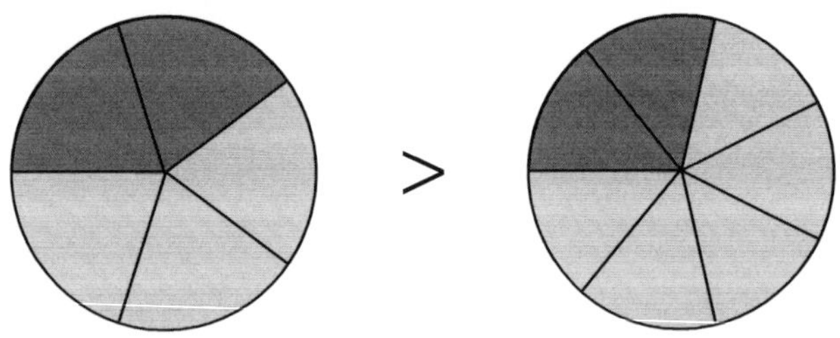

22. D: To calculate when her lunch break finishes, add 30 minutes to the time it starts, 12:15. Since we know that 15 + 30 = 45, the correct answer is 12:45.

23. D: Since each penny has a mass of about 3 grams, you can find the total mass of 6 pennies by adding 3 + 3 + 3 + 3 + 3 + 3. In other words, you have to multiply 3×6. Thus, the total mass is 18 grams.

24. C: To find mass of the leftover piece, subtract the mass you cut off from the mass of the original board: 12 – 4. Thus, the mass of the leftover piece is 8 kg.

25. A: To draw a bar graph, first make a title and two axes. For this problem, the vertical axis will have average yearly rainfall (in inches), and the horizontal axis will have the five given cities. Moreover, notice that the data ranges from 8 in. of rainfall to 50 in. Therefore, for the vertical axis, we can go from 0 to 60 by counting by tens.

Set up the bar graph.

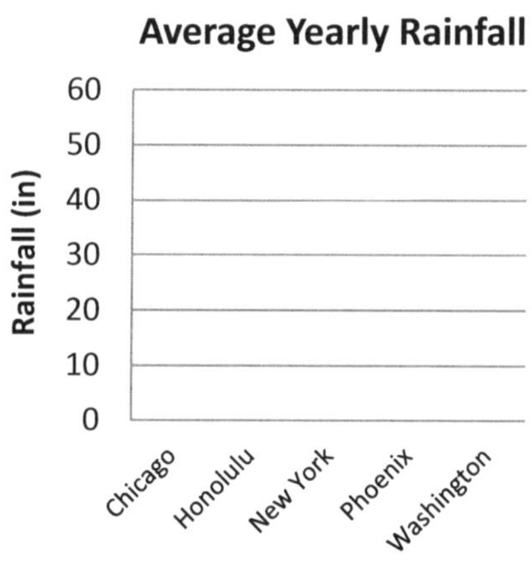

Finally, add a bar for each of the five cities. Using your eye, try to make sure that the bar for Chicago goes up to about 36. Then make a bar for Honolulu that goes up to about 18, and so on.

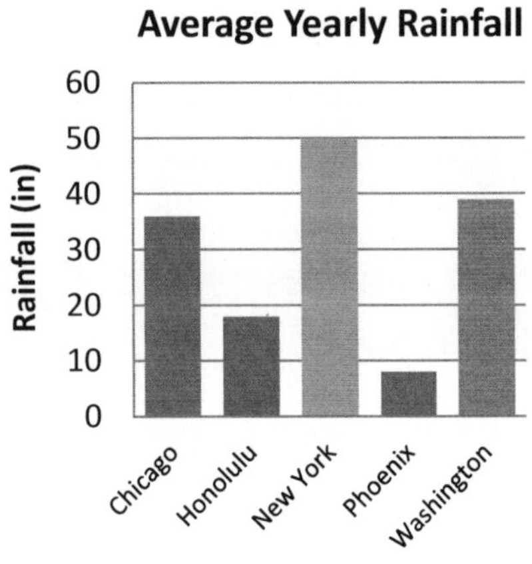

26. B: To draw a line plot, first make a title and two axes. For this problem, the vertical axis will have the four objects, and the horizontal axis will have the length of the objects (in cm). Moreover, notice that the data ranges from 4.1 cm to 10 cm. Therefore, for the vertical axis, we can go from 0 to about 12. Set up the line plot.

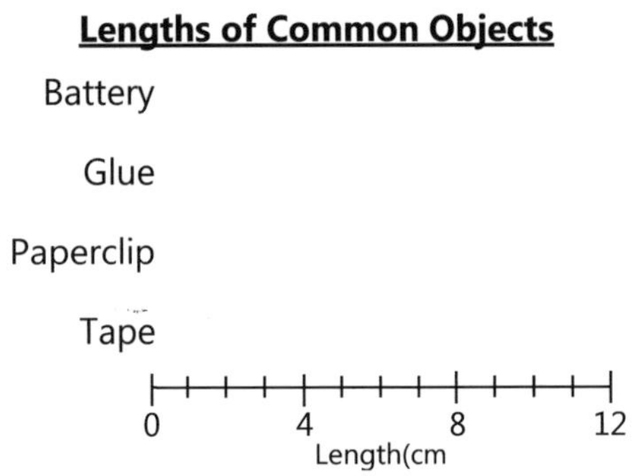

Finally, add ×'s in horizontal lines for each of the four objects. Put one × for each centimeter. For parts of a centimeter (like the ".1" in 4.1), use a portion of an ×.

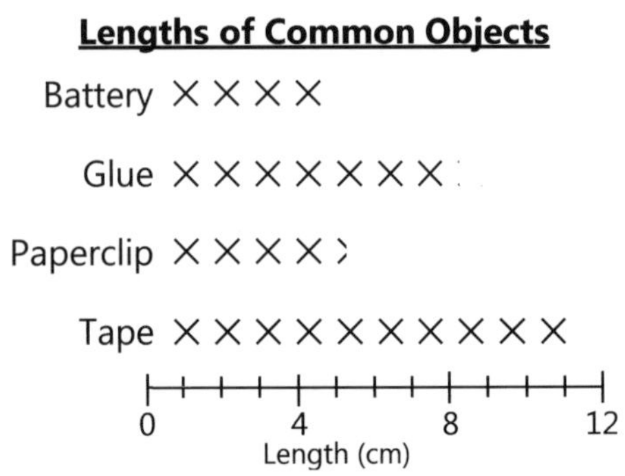

27. C: A square with sides of length 1 unit (called a "unit square") has an area of 1 square unit. Since the sides of the unit square in the problem are 1 cm long, its area is 1 square centimeter, notated as 1 cm^2.

28. D: A figure that is covered with *n* unit squares has an area of *n* square units. Since the given figure is covered with 25 unit squares, its area is 25 square units.

29. D: A figure that is covered with *n* unit squares has an area of *n* square units. Since the given figure is divided into 6 unit squares, its area is 6 square units.

30. C: Notice that the rectangle has already been divided into unit squares. A figure that is divided into *n* unit squares has an area of *n* square units. Therefore, to calculate the area of the rectangle, count or calculate the number of unit squares. Since there are five columns of unit squares and three rows, you can calculate the number of squares by multiplying 5 by 3 to get 15. Thus, the area of the rectangle is 15 square units.

31. B: To calculate the area of a rectangle, multiply its length by its width. For the given rectangle, multiply 2 by 3 to get 6. Thus, the area of the rectangle is 6 square units.

32. D: To calculate the area of a rectangle, multiply its length by its width. For the rectangular check, multiply 3 by 6 to get 18. Thus, the area of the check is 18 in^2.

33. A: Notice that the large rectangle is made of two smaller ones.

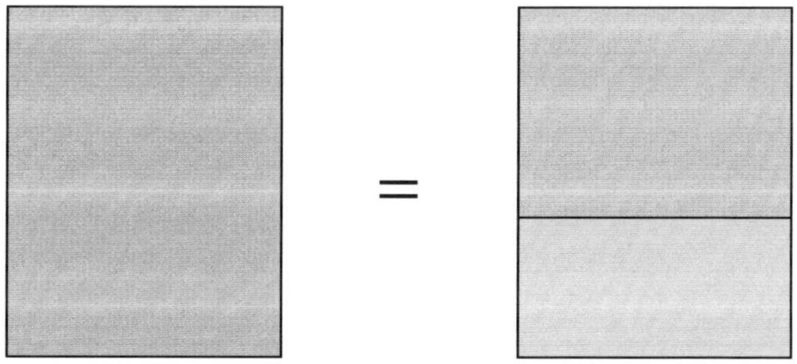

Therefore, the area of the large rectangle is equal to the sum of the areas of the smaller ones.

Large rectangle = Small rectangle + Small rectangle

To calculate the area of a rectangle, multiply its length by its width. The length of the large rectangle is 4, and its width is 3 + 2. Therefore, its area is $4 \times (3 + 2)$. In the same way, we find that the areas of the two small rectangles are 4×3 and 4×2. Thus, the figure represents the equation below.

$$4 \times (3 + 2) = (4 \times 3) + (4 \times 2)$$

34. B: Break up the given figure into two rectangles. If necessary, find the length of any new sides.

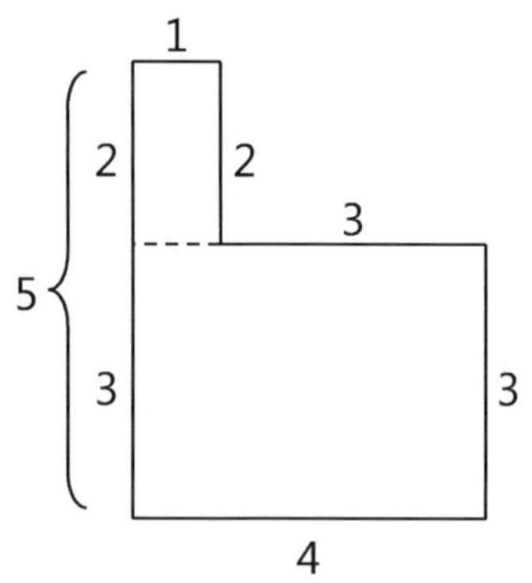

Now find the areas of the two rectangles by multiplying their lengths and their widths. Since the top rectangle is 1 unit by 2 units, its area is 2 square units. The bottom rectangle is 4 units by 3 units, so its area is 12 square units. Therefore, the area of the whole figure is 2 + 12 = 14 square units.

35. A: Break up the given figure into three rectangles. If necessary, find the lengths of any new sides.

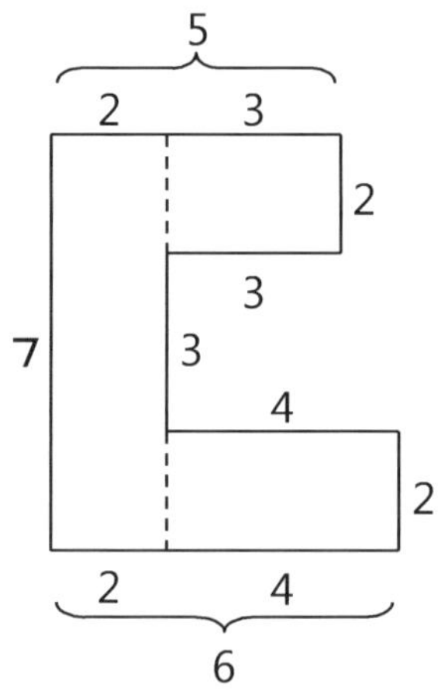

Now find the areas of the three rectangles by multiplying their length times their width. Since the top rectangle is 3 units by 2 units, its area is 6 square units. The left rectangle is 2 units by 7 units, so its area is 14 square units. The bottom rectangle is 4 units by 2 units, so its area is 8 square units. Therefore, the area of the whole figure is 6 + 14 + 8 = 28 square units.

36. A: First draw a picture of the rectangle.

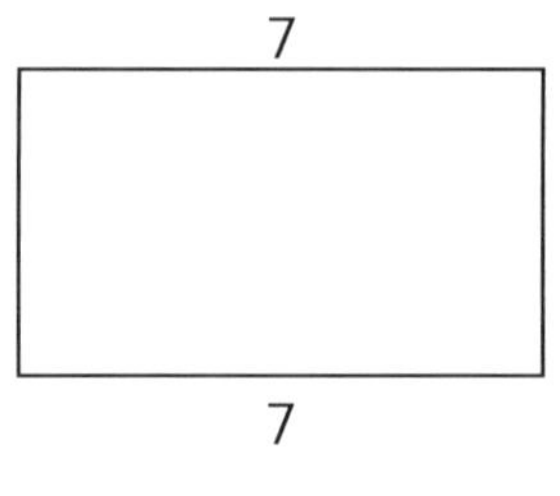

The perimeter of a rectangle is the sum of all of its side lengths. The perimeter of the rectangle is given as 22 units. Therefore, if we add (width + 7 + width + 7), the result will be 22.The only way this can happen is if the width is 4 units.

$$4 + 7 + 4 + 7 = 22$$

37. B: Carefully examine the three figures. Notice that all three sides of the equilateral triangle have the same lengths, all four sides of the square have the same lengths, and all five sides of the regular polygon have the same lengths. On the other hand, only the square has right angles. And only the triangle has three sides.

38. A: If a shape is partitioned (divided) into *n* parts of equal area, then the area of each part is $\frac{1}{n}$ of the whole. The given square is divided into 9 parts with equal areas, and one part is shaded. Therefore, the shaded area is $\frac{1}{9}$ of the total area.

Practice Test #2

Answers and Explanations

1. D: You can think of 8×5 as eight groups of five objects. If you save \$5 a week for 8 weeks straight, then the total amount of money you have saved is \$5 + \$5 + \$5 + \$5 + \$5 + \$5 + \$5 + \$5, which is eight groups of \$5.

2. A: You can think of $36 \div 6$ as equally dividing 36 objects into six groups. If 36 crayons are divided among 6 students, then each student gets six crayons.

3. D: There are 3 groups with 6 cans each. Therefore, you can find the total number of cans by multiplying 3×6. The result is 18 cans.

4. C: The opposite of division is multiplication. Use multiplication of the quotient (7) and divisor (□) to obtain a multiplication problem.
$7 \times \square = 28$.
The opposite of multiplication is division. Use division of the product (28) by the known factor (7) to obtain the missing number.
$28 \div 7 = 4$
Therefore, the missing number is 4.

5. B: The commutative property of multiplication states that the order of the numbers being multiplied does not matter. For instance, 2×3 and 3×2 are both equal to 6. In the problem, we are given the equation $14 \times 11 = 154$. Therefore, by the commutative property, 11×14 is also equal to 154.

6. C: Division and multiplication are inverse operations just as subtraction and addition are. To calculate $7 - 3$, ask yourself "What number can be added to 3 to get 7?" Since the answer is 4, we know that $7 - 3 = 4$.

Similarly, to calculate $30 \div 5$, ask yourself "What number can be multiplied by 5 to get 30?" By trial-and-error, you can find that $6 \times 5 = 30$. Therefore, we know that $30 \div 5 = 6$.

7. C: In the multiplication table, the 9s are 9, 18, 27, 36, 45, 54, 63, 72, 81, 90. Therefore, $9 \times 9 = 81$.

8. D: To start, let the letter *a* stand for the number of shirts Steve had before Christmas (which is what we are looking for). Now we can say that after he gets 3 shirts for Christmas, Steve has a total of $a + 3$ shirts. We are also told that he has 12 shirts now. Therefore, the correct equation is $a + 3 = 12$.

Because addition and subtraction are related, we can calculate *a* by subtracting $12 - 3$. The answer is 9, which we can check by making sure that $9 + 3 = 12$. It works, so Steve had a total of 9 shirts before Christmas.

9. B: To start, let the letter *b* stand for the number of chocolates in the box at the beginning (which is what we are looking for). Now we can say that if the chocolates are distributed among six people, each person gets $b \div 6$ chocolates. We are also told that each person gets 4 chocolates. Therefore, the correct equation is $b \div 6 = 4$.

Because multiplication and division are related, we can calculate *b* by multiplying 4×6. The answer is 24, which we can check by making sure that $24 \div 6 = 4$. It works, so there were 24 chocolates in the box in the beginning.

10. A: Carefully examine the addition table and identify some of the sums that are even. Notice that if both numbers are odd, then the result is always even. For instance:

$$1 + 7 = 8$$
$$3 + 3 = 6$$
$$3 + 9 = 12$$
$$7 + 5 = 12$$

11. A: To round to the nearest hundred, first look at the digit in the hundreds place, which is an 8. Thus, if you round 834 *down*, the 8 will stay the same, and the answer will be 800. Conversely, if you round it *up*, the 8 will go up to a 9, and the answer will be 900. Finally, look at the number after the 8, which is a 3. Since it is less than 5, you should round down. Therefore, the answer is 800.

12. B: Set up the addition vertically, making sure to line up the digits by place value.

$$\begin{array}{r} 39 \\ \underline{+\ 464} \\ 503 \end{array}$$

13. C: Notice that 50 is a multiple of 10; in other words, it has a zero in the ones place. There is a trick to multiplying numbers like this. To multiply 50×7, first multiply 5×7 and then add a zero to the end. Therefore, the answer is 350.

14. A: A fraction $\frac{1}{b}$ can be represented as a whole partitioned (or divided) into *b* equal parts. For example, if a figure is divided into 2 equal parts, then each part represents $\frac{1}{2}$ of the whole. Notice that the circle in the problem is divided into 6 equal parts and one of those parts is shaded. Therefore, it represents the fraction $\frac{1}{6}$.

15. A: If you partition (or divide) the space between 0 and 1 on a number line into b equal parts, then each part has size $\frac{1}{b}$ and the right side of the first division represents the point $\frac{1}{b}$. For example, if you divide the space between 0 and 1 on a number line into three equal parts, then each part has size $\frac{1}{3}$, and the first endpoint represents the point $\frac{1}{3}$.

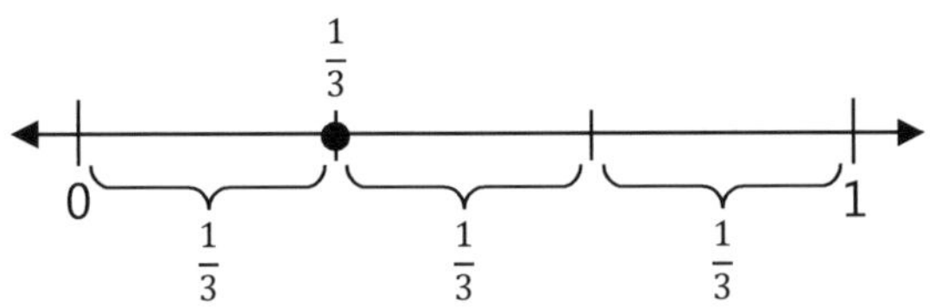

Therefore, to find $\frac{1}{5}$, divide the space between 0 and 1 on a number line into five equal parts. The first endpoint represents $\frac{1}{5}$.

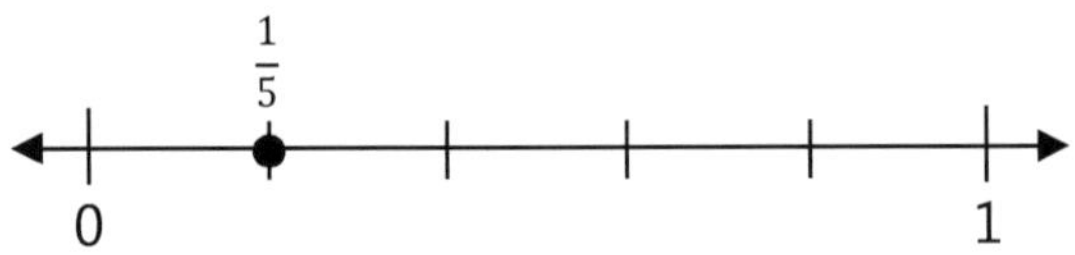

16. D: If you partition (or divide) the space between 0 and 1 on a number line into b equal parts, then the ath division to the right of zero is the point $\frac{a}{b}$. For example, if you divide the space between 0 and 1 on a number line into three equal parts, then the second endpoint represents the point $\frac{2}{3}$.

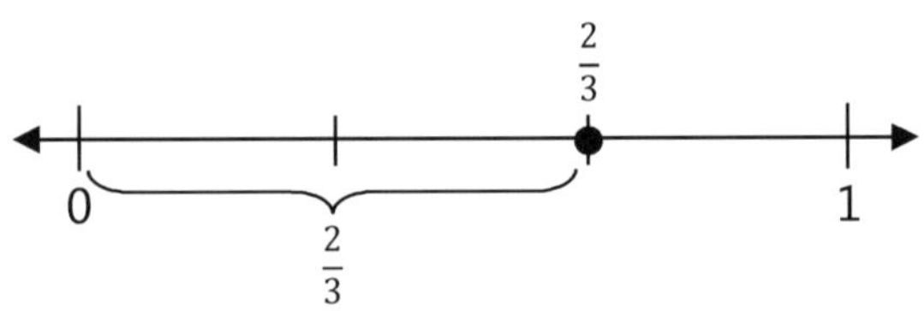

Therefore, to find $\frac{3}{4}$, divide the space between 0 and 1 on the number line into four equal parts. The third endpoint represents $\frac{3}{4}$.

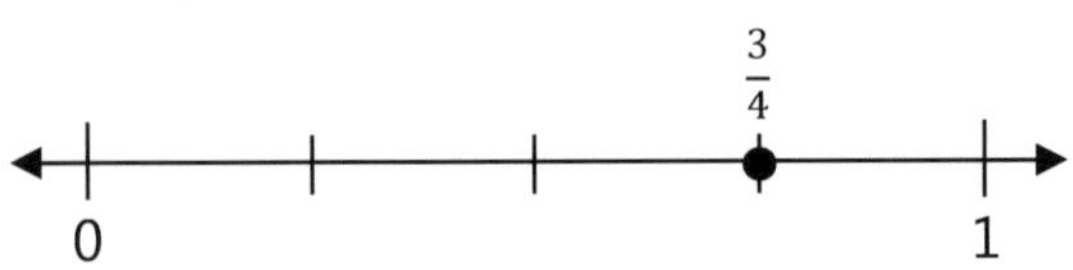

17. B: A fraction can be represented as a whole partitioned (or divided) into equal parts. In addition, two fractions are equivalent if they are the same size. Notice that the rectangle in the problem is divided into 8 equal parts and that two of those parts are shaded. Therefore, the shaded portion represents $\frac{2}{8}$. This is equivalent to the fraction $\frac{1}{4}$ as shown by the darkly shaded area in the rectangles below.

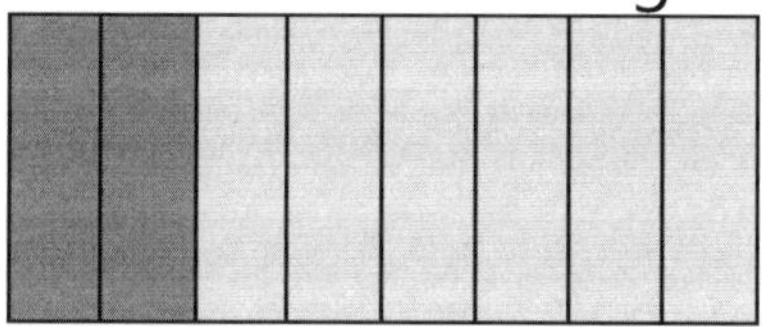

=

18. C: A fraction can be represented as a whole partitioned (or divided) into equal parts. In addition, two fractions are equivalent if they are the same size. The darkly shaded area below represents the fraction $\frac{6}{10}$.

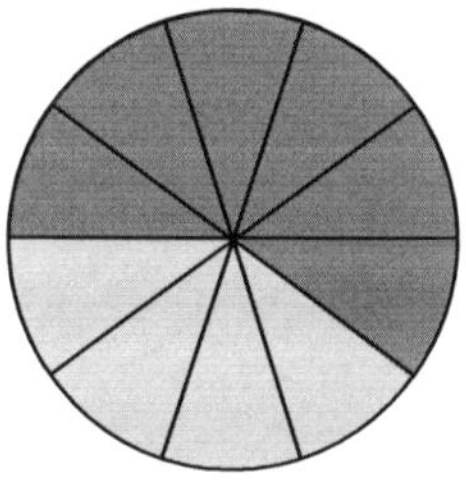

This is equivalent to the fraction $\frac{3}{5}$ as shown by the darkly shaded area below.

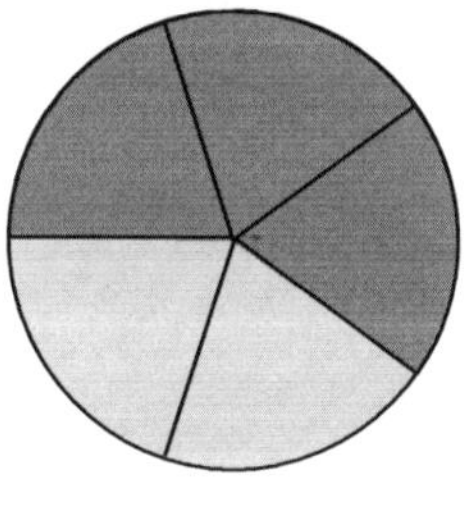

19. D: A whole number *a* can be expressed as a fraction $\frac{a}{1}$. This is because $\frac{a}{1}$ represents *a* "divided" into one part. Therefore, 3 is equivalent to the fraction $\frac{3}{1}$.

20. C: A fraction $\frac{a}{b}$ can be represented as *a* parts of a whole that is partitioned (or divided) into *b* equal parts. Therefore, if you divide a whole into 8 parts, then 3 of those parts are smaller than 5 of them. Thus, the correct answer is $\frac{3}{8} < \frac{5}{8}$ as shown by the figures below.

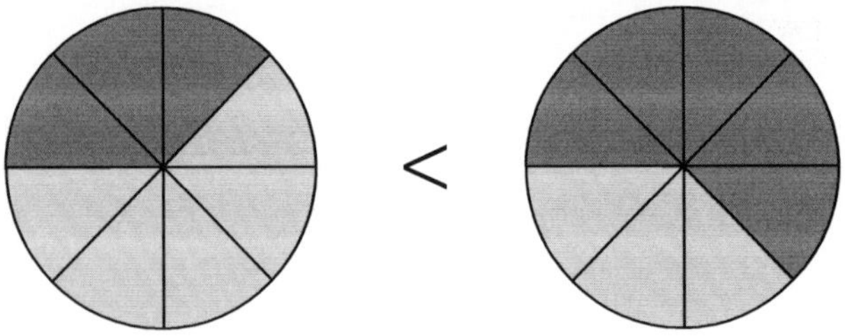

21. A: A fraction $\frac{a}{b}$ can be represented as *a* parts of a whole that is partitioned (or divided) into *b* equal parts. Therefore, if you divide a whole into 6 parts, then each part will be larger than if you had divided the whole into 8 parts. Thus, the correct answer is $\frac{5}{6} > \frac{5}{8}$ as shown by the figures below.

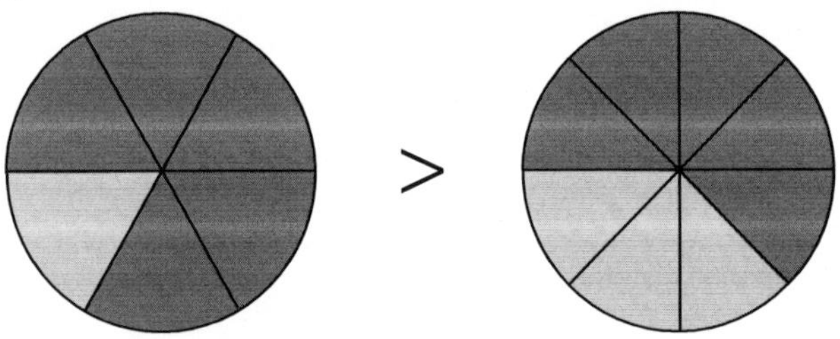

22. B: To calculate when the show begins, subtract 25 minutes from the time it ends, 3:40. Since we know that 40 – 25 = 15, the correct answer is 3:15.

23. B: To find the volume of soda left, subtract the amount the guests drank from the amount you had at the beginning: 12 – 8. Thus, there are 4 liters of soda left.

24. A: Since the quarters all have the same mass, you can find mass of each one by dividing the total mass by the number of coins. Since the total mass is 15 grams and there are 3 quarters, divide 15 ÷ 3. Thus, each quarter has a mass of about 5 grams.

25. B: To draw a bar graph, first make a title and two axes. For this problem, the vertical axis will have average monthly temperature (in degrees Fahrenheit), and the horizontal axis will have the four given months. Moreover, notice that the data ranges from 35°F to 72°F. Therefore, for the vertical axis, we can go from 0 to 80 by counting by twenties. Set up the bar graph.

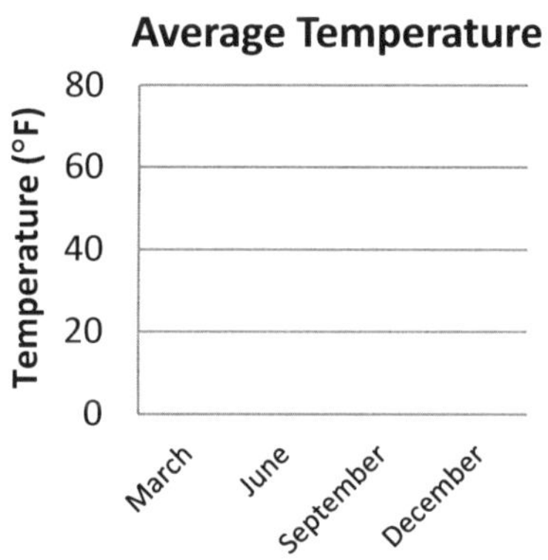

Finally, add a bar for each of the four months. Using your eye, try to make sure that the bar for March goes up to about 41. Then make a bar for June that goes up to about 72, and so on.

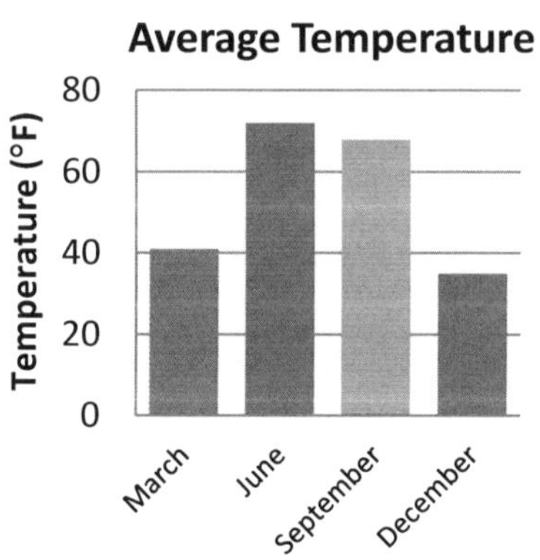

26. D: To draw a line plot, first make a title and two axes. For this problem, the vertical axis will have the four objects, and the horizontal axis will have the length of the objects (in inches). Moreover, notice that the data ranges from 4 in. to 11 in. Therefore, for the vertical axis, we can go from 0 to about 12. Set up the line plot.

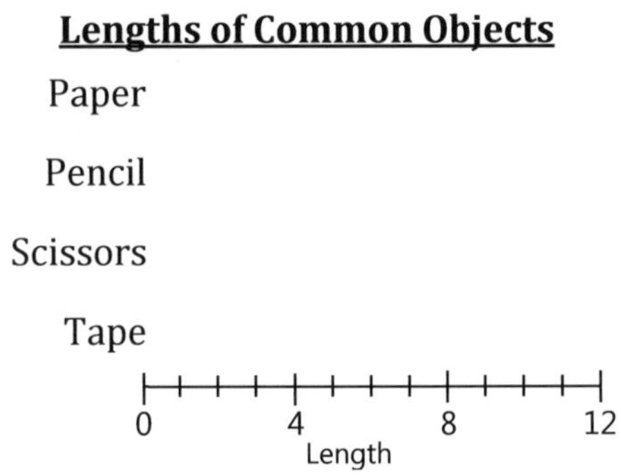

Finally, add ×'s in horizontal lines for each of the four objects. Put one × for each inch. For parts of an inch (like the "½" in 7 ½), use a portion of an ×.

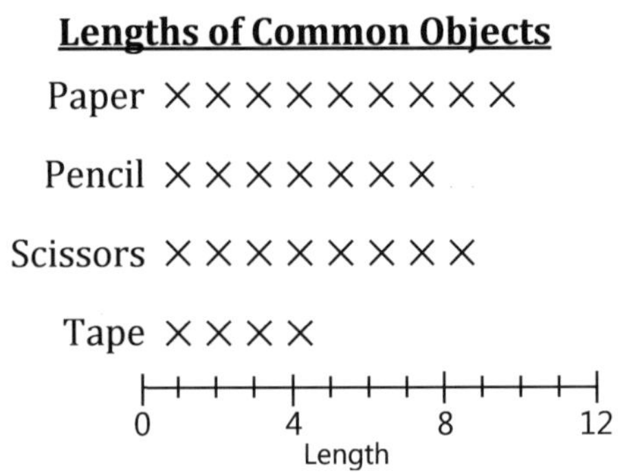

27. C: A square with sides of length 1 unit (called a "unit square") has an area of 1 square unit. Since the sides of the unit square in the problem are 1 ft long, its area is 1 square foot, notated as 1 ft^2.

28. D: A figure that is covered with *n* unit squares has an area of *n* square units. Since the given figure is covered with 16 unit squares, its area is 16 square units.

29. D: A figure that is covered with n unit squares has an area of n square units. Since the given figure is divided into 8 unit squares, its area is 8 square units.

30. A: Notice that the rectangle has already been divided into unit squares. A figure that is divided into n unit squares has an area of n square units. Therefore, to calculate the area of the rectangle, count or calculate the number of unit squares. Since there are three columns of unit squares and four rows, you can calculate the number of squares by multiplying 3 by 4 to get 12. Thus, the area of the rectangle is 12 square units.

31. B: To calculate the area of a rectangle, multiply its length by its width. For the given rectangle, multiply 4 by 2 to get 8. Thus, the area of the rectangle is 8 square units.

32. D: To calculate the area of a rectangle, multiply its length by its width. For the rectangular postcard, multiply 3 by 5 to get 15. Thus, the area of the postcard is 15 in^2.

33. D: Notice that the large rectangle is made of two smaller ones.

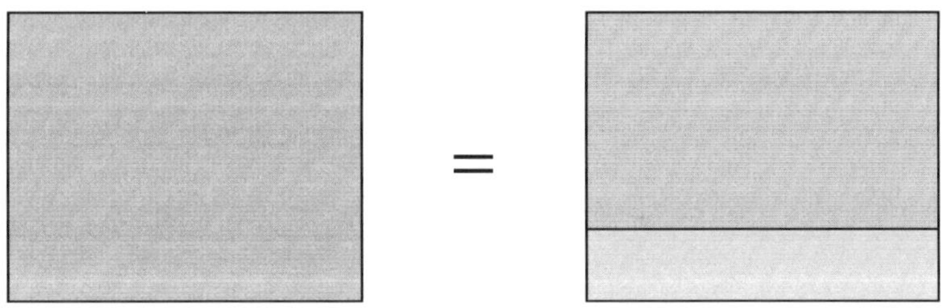

Therefore, the area of the large rectangle is equal to the sum of the areas of the smaller ones.

Large rectangle = Small rectangle + Small rectangle

To calculate the area of a rectangle, multiply its length by its width. The length of the large rectangle is 5, and its width is 3 + 1. Therefore, its area is

$5 \times (3 + 1)$. In the same way, we find that the areas of the two small rectangles are 5×3 and 5×1. Thus, the figure represents the equation below.

$$5 \times (3 + 1) = (5 \times 3) + (5 \times 1)$$

34. A: Break up the given figure into two rectangles.

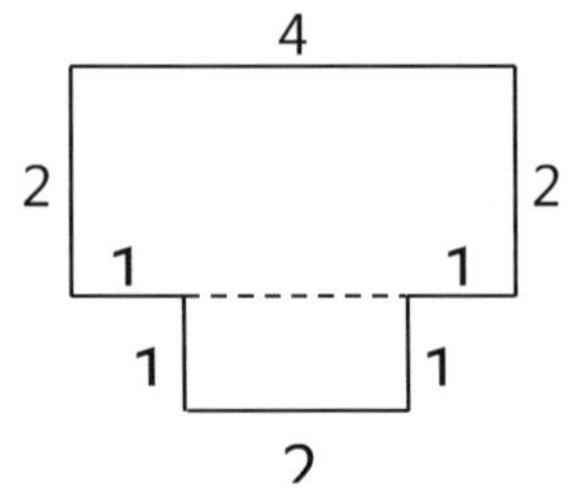

Now find the areas of the two rectangles by multiplying their length times their width. Since the top rectangle is 4 units by 2 units, its area is 8 square units. The bottom rectangle is 2 units by 1 unit, so its area is 2 square units. Therefore, the area of the whole figure is $8 + 2 = 10$ square units.

35. C: Break up the given figure into three rectangles. If necessary, find the lengths of any new sides.

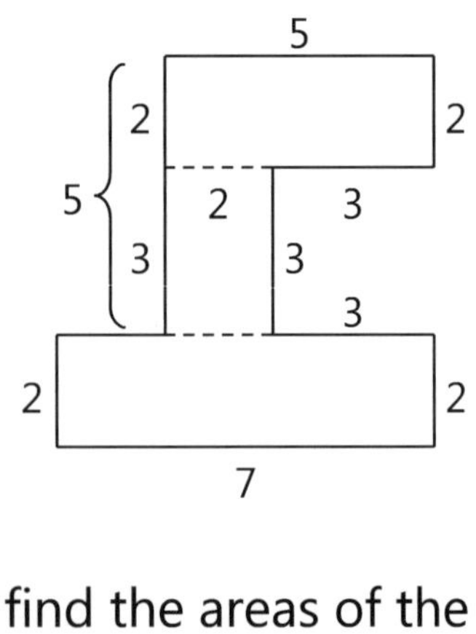

Now find the areas of the three rectangles by multiplying their lengths by their widths. Since the top rectangle is 5 units by 2 units, its area is 10 square units. The middle rectangle is 2 units by 3 units, so its area is 6

square units. The bottom rectangle is 7 units by 2 units, so its area is 14 square units. Therefore, the area of the whole figure is 10 + 6 + 14 = 30 square units.

36. D: First draw a picture of the yard.

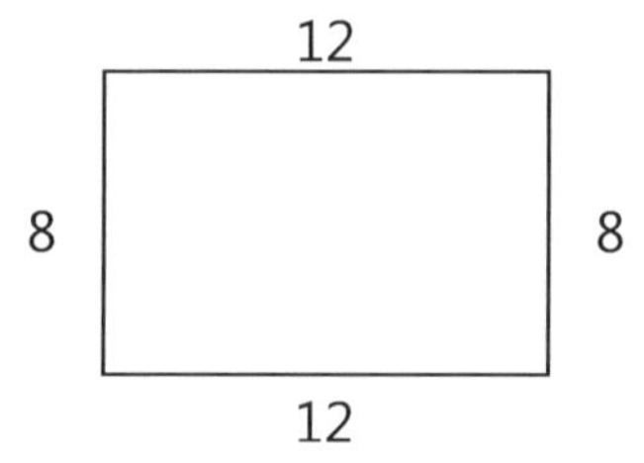

To find the amount of fencing James needs, add the lengths of the four sides of the rectangle. This is called the perimeter of the rectangle.

$$8 + 12 + 8 + 12 = 40$$

Therefore, James should get 40 yards of fencing.

37. A: Carefully examine the three figures. Notice that they are all quadrilaterals; that is, they all have four sides. On the other hand, only the square has right angles. And only the rhombus and the square have sides of equal length.

38. A: If a shape is partitioned (divided) into *n* parts of equal area, then the area of each part is $\frac{1}{n}$ of the whole. The given triangle is divided into four parts with equal areas, and one part is shaded. Therefore, the shaded area is $\frac{1}{4}$ of the total area.

Online Resources

Due to our efforts to try to keep this book to a manageable length, we've created a link that will give you access to all of your online resources:

mometrix.com/resources719/ssmcag3mathwb

It's Your Moment, Let's Celebrate It!

Share your story @mometrixtestpreparation